Word Smugglers

A Story of Resistance in the Warsaw Ghetto

By Amy McDonald

In memory of my uncle,
Lieutenant Colonel William L. McDonald...
World War II veteran, historian, pastor,
and the first author in our family.

And

In memory of Max Steinmetz, Holocaust survivor.
My teacher, my mentor, my champion,
my hero... my friend.

Acknowledgements

First and foremost, I am profoundly grateful to Sam Kassow, author of *Who Will Write Our History*, for his help with this book. His historical expertise, input, and guidance were my teachers. I was touched and humbled by his patience and kindness.

Thank you to Deborah Layman for extensively reviewing and editing the manuscript. I am thankful for your input and generosity of spirit.

As always, thank you to my family, friends, and colleagues who spent time reading and editing the manuscript. But more than anything, thank you for your unending and unfailing love and support.

Foreword

Before his death in Majdanek in 1943, the Jewish historian Isaac Schipper, one of Ringelblum's mentors observed that "what we know about murdered peoples is usually what their killers choose to say about them." His student, the communal activist and scholar Dr. Emanuel Ringelblum was determined that the killers not have the final say. In a heroic and desperate war for memory, his archive became a symbol of cultural resistance. The courageous band of comrades that he brought together in the archive buried time capsules, stuffed with documents, drawings and photographs, that foiled the Germans' determination to distort and pervert the memory of their Jewish victims. Of the 60 or so members of the Oyneg Shabes only three survived. One of those survivors, Rachel Auerbach, made the mordant comment that the archive had better luck saving paper than it had in saving people.

Had this archive disappeared forever, historians of Polish Jewry in the Holocaust would have had little more than German documents, various Polish sources and a few survivor memoirs. Scholars could certainly have written about the perpetrators or about Polish attitudes towards the Jews. But what they could not have done was to write anything meaningful about the inner life of the Jews themselves. The murdered Jews of Poland would have remained a mass of anonymous victims, without names, without identity and without a record of what little agency they may have possessed. Of course survivors would have written their memoirs and given their testimonies. But those accounts would have reflected what they knew after the event, not Jewish voices in real time. The testimony of those who survived mass murder was quite different from the words of those who still did not know the final outcome, who were still living in communities that were not yet destroyed.

Beginning in the 1970's, many superb studies have appeared about various aspects of Warsaw Jewry in World War II. One need only cite the works of Ruta Sakowska, Israel Gutman, Havi Dreifuss, Jacek Leociak, Barbara Engelking, Katarzyna Person, Leah Preiss or the more controversial but still useful monograph of Gunnar S. Paulsson. But without the Ringelblum archive, it is hard to see how most of these books could have been written. Without the archive, what could we have known about the inner life of the ghetto: social conflicts, folklore, Jewish reactions to the tightening Nazi vise, the attitudes of intellectuals, religious life, economic conditions, resistance?

Had it not been for the Oyneg Shabes, we would never have read some of the most sophisticated and poignant examples of Jewish religious thought in modern times, the ghetto sermons of Rabbi Kalonymous Shapiro. They were all hidden in the second cache of the archive. Nor would we have known much about the massive underground ghetto press which provided a fascinating window into the political life of the ghetto, what people knew and when, how news from the outside reached the Jews trapped inside. More than 90% of these underground papers survived only because of the archive. These newspapers alone run to more than 3000 pages. The diaries of Emanuel Ringelblum and Abraham Shapiro, the brilliant reportage of Peretz Opoczynski, the writings of Rabbi Shimon Huberband and much much more would have vanished forever.

Ringelblum imbued all of his associates with his deep faith in the mission of the archive. As the 17-year-old David Graber helped bury the first cache of documents on August 3, 1942, he wrote a last letter. In it he tried to imagine the moment when those time capsules would surface and "scream the truth at the world." Then he and his comrades would enjoy a posthumous victory. The world would be moved and shocked. And he and his friends would become the "fathers, the teachers, the educators of the future." Another member of the archive, Gustawa Jarecka, hoped that her words would be like "a stone under history's wheel", a call on the world's conscience to change the direction of history away from barbarism and towards decency.

In writing this book, aimed at a young audience, Amy McDonald reminds us to focus on the human dimension of the Oyneg Shabes. These 60 people included teenagers like David Graber and Nahum Grzywacz, remarkable women like Rachel Auerbach and Gustawa Jarecka, teachers, rabbis, businessmen. Communists worked alongside religious Jews, people who would never have spoken to each other before the war buried the hatchet in order to gather and conceal material. Those who risked their lives to "scream the truth at the world" were not larger than life heroes but ordinary people who understood that in the right circumstances the pen could become a powerful weapon. They desperately wanted to survive. But in the face of death they never flinched from doing their duty to Ringelblum and to history.

This book, *Word Smugglers: A Story of Resistance in the Warsaw Ghetto,* also reminds us that what happened in the Holocaust is not only a Jewish story but an assault on the very idea of our humanity. A modern state mobilized every branch of its bureaucracy and military to define a particular group of people, rob them of their possessions, segregate them and then murder them in death factories and in killing pits. As the last of the survivors pass on, books like these help tell a story that should never be forgotten.

Professor Sam Kassow
Charles Northam Professor of History
at Trinity College in Hartford, CT
Author of *Who Will Write Our History:*
Rediscovering a Hidden Archive
from the Warsaw Ghetto

Author's Note

This was a very different type of story to write. It is based on actual events and actual people. However, because of the nature of the fate of the Jews in the Warsaw Ghetto, only fragments are known about certain aspects of the characters' lives. In some instances, all we know about them is what was written and saved within the Oyneg Shabes Archive. The following is a list of characters in this book:

Emanuel Ringelblum: Polish Jewish historian, teacher, Jewish aid worker, and creator of the Oyneg Shabes archive. Much is known and documented about his family, career and experiences in the Warsaw Ghetto.

Rachel Auerbach: writer, director of one of the many soup kitchens in the ghetto, and member of the Oyneg Shabes Archive. Much is known and documented about her family, career, and experiences in the Warsaw Ghetto.

Israel Lichtenstein: teacher and principal at a Jewish school, Jewish aid worker, and member of the Oyneg Shabes Archive. Much is known and documented about his family, career, and experiences in the Warsaw Ghetto.

David Graber: teenager, former student of Israel Lichtenstein, and member of the Oyneg Shabes Archive. All that is known about his life is what was discovered within the Oyneg Shabes Archive. His family members in this story are fictionalized.

Nahum Grzywacz: teenager, former student of Israel Lichtenstein, and member of the Oyneg Shabes Archive. All that is known about his life is what was discovered in the Archive. His family members in this story are fictionalized.

POLAND 1933

0   100

MILES

Baltic
Sea

GERMANY

DANZIG

Bydgoszcz

Oder

Berlin

Zbaszyn

Poznan

Warta

Elbe

Oder

Piotrkow
Trybunalski

Leipzig

Dresden

Breslau

N

Prague

Kra

CZECHOSLOVAKIA

Brno

Munich

Danube

Vienna

Linz

Bratislava

United States Holocaust Memorial Museum

INTRODUCTION

On September 1, 1939, Germany unleashed its Nazi blitzkrieg on the country of Poland. World War II in Europe had begun. German troops and tanks raced to surround and capture the city of Warsaw, the capital of Poland. German planes pounded Warsaw with bombs. The citizens of Warsaw began digging shelter trenches on city streets for protection.

For the next few weeks, radio broadcasts reported the fall of one Polish city after another. Refugees from these cities streamed into Warsaw, hoping to outrun the advancing German army. The residents of Warsaw continued to hold out hope as the Polish military fought bravely on. Air raid alarms sounded daily and the streets of Warsaw emptied as deafening bombs exploded overhead. Terrified families and neighbors huddled together in cellars, shelters, courtyards, and stairwells. The ground and buildings shook as if it were an earthquake. Schools, train stations, banks, and stores closed. Hundreds of people stood in long lines to get a loaf of bread. People began searching for potatoes in fields.

On September 13, 1939, Warsaw was surrounded. No one was allowed to enter or leave the city. Water was shut off and electricity was damaged. It had taken the German army less than one month to conquer Poland.

Before World War II, Warsaw had a population of approximately 1.3 million people. The city was not only the capital of Poland, but also a major center of Jewish life and culture. The Jewish community of Warsaw was the second largest in the world, second only to New York City. While the German occupation of Poland was bad for all Polish citizens, it was especially bad for Polish Jews. Jewish schools were shut down. Jewish businesses were taken over by the German authorities. Jews in Warsaw were required to wear a white armband with a blue Star of David for identification.

In October 1940, the Jewish community in Warsaw learned the horrible news that they would have to move into a designated area of the city known as a ghetto. The ghetto was enclosed by a brick wall that was over ten feet high with barbed wire and glass on top. Inside the ghetto, there was massive overcrowding, hunger, disease, and cruelty.

This is not just a story about the German invasion of Poland or the Warsaw Ghetto. It is a story within a story. This is a story about a courageous group of men, women, and young people who chose to resist and fight back against cruelty and fear. This group did not fight back with guns and weapons. They fought back with words, stories, and truth.

ONE

September 13, 1939
Warsaw, Poland

The air raid sirens screamed as David ran furiously down Wolynska Street. He was trying to make it home before the next round of bombs fell. He was almost there and could see his father waiting at the entrance to the air raid shelter. Sixteen-year-old David Graber lived with his parents, Henryk and Leah, and ten-year-old sister, Abigail, in a small apartment at 21 Wolynska Street, located in one of the poorest Jewish sections of Warsaw. "I was about to come looking for you," his father said, as they descended into the shelter. The worried look on his mother's face eased when David and his father entered the underground cellar.

"Nahum and I were helping dig tank trenches," David said, as he sat down on the ground beside his mother.

"I'm not surprised, but I was worried sick," she replied, as she pulled him and Abigail close to her. The walls shook as the explosions began.

David and 15-year-old Nahum Grzywacz had been best friends since elementary school. They both attended the Borochov School on 68 Nowolipki Street through the sixth grade. Since their apartment buildings were only a couple of blocks apart, they walked back and forth to school together almost every day. Nahum lived with his

Destroyed buildings in Warsaw following a German aerial attack. September 1939.
United States Holocaust Memorial Museum.

parents, Benjamin and Chaya, and his six-year-old brother, Samuel, at 87 Gesia Street, on a street crowded with old, run-down apartment buildings.

For the past five days, German tanks had attempted to roll in and crush Warsaw. They were pushed back by the Polish military. The Germans then began to attack Warsaw from the air. The Polish air force fought off the Luftwaffe, the German air force, as long as they could.

The city was being bombed almost daily. On September 13, the Luftwaffe targeted the Jewish sections of Warsaw. It was the first day of Rosh Hashanah, the Jewish New Year.

Like David, Nahum barely made it home before the new wave of bombs began hitting the Jewish sections of town. As he rushed into his apartment building, Nahum spotted Mr. and Mrs. Stern, his elderly neighbors, struggling to make their way down the stairs. "Let me help you, Mrs. Stern," Nahum said, as he slowed down and offered her his arm. Mr. Stern followed close behind as they made their way to the basement of their apartment building. Nahum saw that his mother, Chaya, and brother, Samuel, were already huddled in the crowded basement with many of their neighbors. But he did not see his father.

"Mama, where's Papa?" he shouted over the noise of panicked people.

"Nahum, I was so worried! You were supposed to be back over an hour ago. And your Papa went to check on Grandma and Grandpa. He's not back yet." Just as she spoke, the muffled thudding of the bombs began. Plaster and dust drifted like snow from the ceiling as the explosions came closer.

The bombing seemed to go on forever. When it finally stopped, David and his family, along with the others, slowly emerged from the shelter. All of the street lamps were out and there was no electricity, but the blackness of the night was illuminated by raging fires.

"Papa, look!" David shouted as he pointed at the buildings down the street. Fire streaked and billowed out of windows, and the air was hot and smoky. David and his father joined a bucket brigade of volunteers who passed water down the line to try and slow down the spread of the fires. Many families could only stand and watch as their apartments and belongings were destroyed. Where would they go? What would they do?

A few blocks away, the situation was the same on Nahum's street. And street after street after street. Rescuers dug with shovels, even their bare hands, trying to pull out people trapped beneath the rubble. Ambulances and horse-drawn wagons drove constantly through the streets, carrying the wounded to hospitals. After hours of moving bricks and carrying buckets of water, Nahum, weary with exhaustion, saw his father emerge from the smoke. It had taken Benjamin almost all night to navigate the streets with his elderly parents and get them to safety.

The dim sunrise revealed blocks of charred and smoldering buildings. Nahum and David's families were among the fortunate ones. They still had a home for now. The new day brought even more determination to defend the city. Food supplies began to run low.

"Mama," David said urgently, "I'm going to go check on Nahum." Leah knew it was useless to tell him not to go.

"Stay near the buildings and don't stay gone long," she replied, kissing him on the forehead. Before David was halfway there, he saw Nahum running in his direction. They both had the same idea.

"We should go help dig trenches," Nahum said, as he stopped to catch his breath. The boys took off together, with even more determination to help defend the city. Little did they know what was in store for the city of Warsaw and the people who lived there...especially the Jews. The Germans were coming.

Polish children wander through the ruins of Warsaw after a German bombing. Warsaw, Poland, ca. 1939. United States Holocaust Memorial Museum.

Israel Lichtenstein. Courtesy of the Jewish Historical Institute in Warsaw, Poland.

TWO

September 25, 1939
Warsaw, Poland

Israel Lichtenstein stood in the doorway of the Borochov School at 68 Nowolipki Street. It was late afternoon and the bombs and artillery fire had been falling constantly since early morning. Between bombings, Israel, his wife, Gele, and others taking refuge in the basement, came up quickly for air. The air was heavy with smoke and dust, but it was better than sitting in the cramped and crowded basement and stairwells. The siege of Warsaw was entering its third week. The Germans had cut off the water and gas supply to the city. Food was running out.

Israel was the principal at the Borochov School. A few weeks earlier, he and several other teachers set up a soup kitchen in the school's basement for children and refugees. Before the war, Israel was a member of CENTOS, the Central Organization for the Care of Orphans. Since this organization focused on taking care of people who needed help, Israel had experience with this work and jumped into action. He searched for and collected food, blankets, and clothing that could be used in the soup kitchen.

When the attack on Warsaw began several weeks earlier, the school became not just a place for children to learn, but also a place for families and neighbors to gather. Thousands of refugees streamed into the city and needed shelter and food. Thousands of others who lived in Warsaw decided it was safer to flee the city and try to outrun the Germans.

The roads were full of cars, horse-drawn wagons, and terrified people. Many people lost their homes and everything they owned in the bombings. The school at 68 Nowolipki began to provide soup and a place to stay for those who were now homeless.

"Everyone back down," Israel yelled as explosions began sounding in other parts of the city. The women and children went first as the men waited until the last minute, cursing the Germans with every breath. Minutes turned into hours in the shelter as the bombs blasted away at Warsaw. Mothers held and tried to rock crying babies. Some smoked cigarettes. Others yelled at them to stop smoking. Some tried to sleep on blankets and pillows they brought from home. Someone played a violin.

Children were everywhere. Israel and Gele, both teachers, had created a children's corner in the basement where they told stories and played games. Gele was also an artist. She gathered paper and pencils from classrooms so the restless children could draw pictures.

"Everyone come closer into the circle," Israel called out to the children. "Sit down and let me tell you a story about a funny little mongoose named Rikki-tikki-tavi." As the adults slept, talked, waited, and worried, the children sat knee-to-knee and listened as Israel began the story.

"He was a mongoose, rather like a little cat in his fur and his tail, but quite like a weasel in his head and in his habits...he could fluff up his tail till it looked like a bottle-brush, and his war-cry, as he scuttled through the long grass was, 'Rikk-tikk-tikki-tikki-tchk!'"

He continued to read as the rumble and roar of German airplanes and guns filled the air like a never-ending thunderstorm. Whole areas of the city were in flames. Bombings continued for two weeks.

When Warsaw surrendered on September 27, 1939, the bombings stopped. People waited nervously to see what would happen next. The next day, the German army marched boldly into Warsaw. The sound of their boots echoed through the streets.

After the September bombings, not one pane of window glass was left in the city of Warsaw. Winter was coming.

THREE

March 1940
Warsaw, Poland

The boredom was the worst...along with the constant hunger. Once the bombings ended and the Germans entered Warsaw, life was centered around wondering what would happen next. David's father, Henryk, had just returned from being gone for almost two months where he had been forced to work in a labor camp.

Soon after they took over Warsaw, the Germans issued new laws directed against the Jews. One of these laws stated that all men and women between the ages of 14 and 60 years of age had to register for forced labor. Henryk, Leah, and David all had to register. This meant that they could be dragged out of the streets or rounded up at any moment to do hard work on German projects like building roads.

Henryk had gone out one day to buy bread and was rounded up suddenly by German soldiers. When he didn't return home, Leah, David's mother, heard from neighbors that there had been a round up near their street. For the next few weeks, Leah barely allowed David to leave the apartment, except for going out in the courtyard. The people in their apartment building, just like other apartment buildings on other streets, gathered constantly in the courtyard to talk, gossip, and share news. Almost everyone was afraid to go past the gate of their courtyard and walk in the streets.

When Henryk finally returned home, he was so sick and thin his family barely recognized him. He told stories of working long hours in the freezing cold with very little food. Henryk slowly began to recover and get stronger.

"Mama," David said firmly, "I am going to start going out to buy bread and food. You stay here and take care of Papa."

"No, David, it is too dangerous," Leah said.

"I'll be careful," David promised. "I know the backstreets and I'll stay off the main streets. You need to stay here with Papa and Abigail. I'll be back before you know it," David said with a smile. He hugged Leah quickly and then was out the door.

David headed for Gesia Street to stand in line to buy bread, but stopped first to visit Nahum. David greeted his friend. "I'm going to buy bread. Want to come with me?"

Chaya, Nahum's mother, had the same fears about her son going out into the streets, but finally allowed him to go as long as the boys promised to stay together.

After waiting for over an hour to buy one loaf of bread, David had an idea. In his courtyard, David had heard that Israel Lichtenstein had started a soup kitchen at their former school. He had been one of their favorite teachers. Even though David and Nahum went to the Borochov School years earlier, they had both stayed in touch with Mr. Lichtenstein through a political youth group known as Yungbor.

Both boys were very active in Yungbor and Mr. Lichtenstein often participated in some of their group activities and meetings. "Let's go see if Mr. Lichtenstein is at the school," David suggested.

Nahum smiled. "Good idea." It was the first time he had smiled in days.

When the boys entered their old school on Nowolipki Street, the sounds of children and the smell of soup led them straight to the basement. The basement was now a combination of a restaurant and kitchen. Children and families sat at several long tables with bowls of soup in front of them, eating and talking.

In the middle of it all stood Mr. Lichtenstein. "David, Nahum," he shouted above the noise. He made his way to them, smiling and shaking their hands warmly. "How are you? How are your families?" Mr. Lichtenstein asked with concern.

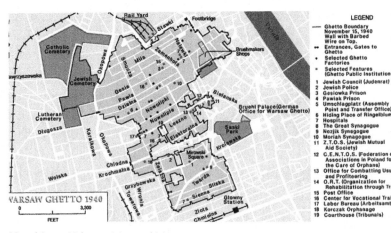

United States Holocaust Memorial Museum.

They each told him the stories of their homes and families since the war began. "I could use some help here at the soup kitchen," Mr. Lichtenstein said. "I could pay you in soup and bread." The boys knew this would really help their families.

"I'll be here tomorrow," David replied.

"Me too," said Nahum.

The boys thanked Mr. Lichtenstein and started to leave, just as another familiar face entered the building. It was Dr. Emanuel Ringelblum, the leader of their Yungbor youth group. He was also a teacher.

After David graduated from school, he worked at a factory. After working all day, he would often attend night classes taught by Dr. Ringelblum. Nahum's family was very poor and he was not able to finish school. He worked for a tailor to make extra money for his family, but also attended the same night classes.

Besides being a wonderful teacher, Dr. Ringelblum also organized hikes and other activities for the students. David and Nahum loved going on the Saturday hikes with their group and Dr. Ringelblum.

Dr. Ringelblum greeted them heartily. "David! Nahum! How good to see you!"

The boys told him that Mr. Lichtenstein had asked them to help in the soup kitchen.

"Excellent," said Dr. Ringelblum. "I'll be seeing you."

David and Nahum were even more excited about working at the soup kitchen. This would be much better than being trapped in their apartments all day.

*An elderly man sells Jewish armbands at the entrance to a building in the Warsaw Ghetto.
United States Holocaust Memorial Museum.*

FOUR

November 1940
Warsaw Ghetto

Emanuel Ringelblum was lost in his thoughts until the German soldier punched him in the mouth. "I beg your pardon, sir," Emanuel quickly said as he took off his hat and bowed. Since the German invasion, all Jews were required to remove their hats and bow when walking past German soldiers. As blood trickled from his mouth, Emanuel thought, "Please keep walking." The soldier continued down the street.

This was only one of many new rules and regulations put in place by the Germans. For months, Jews had not been able to enter certain restaurants or visit public places like libraries or parks. They could not keep more than 2,000 zlotys in cash. They had a curfew and had to be off the streets by 9:00 pm. Jews could not travel by train and when trying to move about the city, they could ride only in Jewish streetcars marked with a yellow star and a sign: For Jews Only. Jews were forced to wear a white armband with a blue Star of David. In movie houses throughout the city,

German propaganda films were shown which portrayed Jews as dirty, carriers of disease, and dangerous parasites.

Before the war, Emanuel was a community organizer who worked for the Joint Distribution Committee, also known as the "Joint." He was also a high school history teacher, historian, and writer. Before the war started, Emanuel Ringelblum was a delegate to the 21st Zionist Congress in Geneva, Switzerland. This meeting was attended by Jews from all over Europe who wanted to create a homeland for the Jews in Palestine. Emanuel returned to Warsaw just as the bombing started and began keeping a detailed journal. He could have fled to escape the city, as many other leaders of the Warsaw Jewish community did, but he chose to stay, step forward, and lead.

The news continued to get worse. The Germans notified the Jews in Warsaw that they would all have to move into a certain part of the city that would be known as the Jewish District, or the ghetto. The ghetto was located in some of the poorest neighborhoods in the city. The Jews moved into the run-down, crowded apartments of the ghetto, which was surrounded by walls patrolled by German soldiers. The Warsaw Ghetto was now sealed and completely cut off from the rest of Warsaw and the outside world. Jews were forbidden to leave the ghetto. Emanuel wrote in his journal, "People in the street didn't know it was going to be a closed ghetto, so it came like a thunderbolt."

Emanuel decided it was time to act. He called a secret meeting and asked a few dozen of his friends and colleagues to attend. His plan was for people throughout the ghetto to begin writing about daily life in the ghetto. They were instructed to write down everything they saw, heard, and experienced. The writings would be collected, hidden, and used later as a historical record of Jewish life and persecution under German occupation. Hopefully, it would serve as evidence against the Germans and the violent crimes they committed.

This would be top-secret, dangerous work. The project was given a code-name: Oyneg Shabes (Joy of the Sabbath). Since Jews gathered on the Sabbath, the group met on Saturdays to avoid suspicion. The members were told to trust no one and remember that secrecy was of the utmost importance.

When World War II began in 1939, Emanuel Ringelblum was 39 years old. His wife, Judyta, was 35 years old and a teacher. They had a son, Uri, who was nine years old.

Jewish youth peer over the wall overlooking Mirowski Plac (Square) that divided the War-saw Ghetto into the small and large ghettos. United States Holocaust Memorial Museum.

FIVE

November 1940
Warsaw Ghetto

It was bitter cold. On the frozen streets of the ghetto, there were crowds of children in ragged clothes and bare feet begging for food. At the soup kitchen at 40 Leszno Street, Rachel Auerbach, the director of the kitchen, smiled as four orphan children burst through the door, knowing that at least here they would get a bowl of soup and piece of bread. It would probably be the only food they ate that day.

"Sit, sit, sit," she said, as she placed a bowl of warm soup in front of each of them.

Rachel Auerbach, a writer and editor in Warsaw before the war, had started the soup kitchen at the request of Emanuel Ringelblum, whom she had met years earlier through his work with the Joint Distribution Committee. On the day the Germans marched boldly into Warsaw, Rachel was making preparations to leave Warsaw when she received a message that her old acquaintance, Emanuel Ringelblum, was looking for her. She was surprised because she and Emanuel did not know each other very well. Curious, Rachel went to Emanuel's office. He thanked her for coming and talked about the German occupation and its consequences for the Jews in Warsaw. He was very concerned about hunger, especially for refugees and orphans. He asked Rachel if she would open and run a soup kitchen.

"Emanuel," she said softly. "I have my ticket and I'm leaving Warsaw tomorrow to join my family."

"We can't all run away," Emanuel said urgently. "We need you here."

Rachel knew that Emanuel was right. Even though she could have escaped the city, Rachel knew then that she would stay in Warsaw.

Gratefully, Emanuel gave Rachel the details regarding the soup kitchen which was to be at 40 Leszno Street, a building that had not been destroyed during the bombings. Rachel immediately got to work. She recruited friends who helped her search through bombed out apartments looking for food, plates, bowls, spoons, and anything else that could be of use in a kitchen. With a few accounting books, a carton of dried plums, half of a sack of rice, and a few packets of dried fish, the soup kitchen began.

The first day the soup kitchen was in operation, Rachel and her staff served 50 bowls of soup. In the ghetto, the kitchen at 40 Leszno Street and other soup kitchens became lifelines for the starving Jewish population. Within two years, the kitchen at 40 Leszno Street would be serving over 2,000 meals a day.

When World War II began in 1939, Rachel Auerbach was 36 years old.

SIX

February 1941
Warsaw Ghetto

Emanuel checked his watch as he hurried through the crowded ghetto streets. He was late for a meeting. As head of the Public Sector of the Aleynhilf, (Jewish Self-Help Society), Emanuel was in charge of all of the house committees in the ghetto. The house committees served as one of the most important community groups in the ghetto.

Before the war, Jewish neighborhoods in Warsaw contained many large apartment buildings. These crowded apartment buildings had their own inner courtyards which often contained small shops, businesses, and places for residents to gather. Anyone who wanted to enter a courtyard from the street had to pass through a gate, which was guarded by a gatekeeper. This made the people living there feel safe.

When World War II started and during the German attack on Warsaw, the courtyards provided Warsaw Jews with a community of neighbors who helped each other.

Photograph found in Ringelblum Archive. Courtesy of the Jewish Historical Institute in Warsaw, Poland.

Neighbors who did not know each other before the war now shared food and took care of each other's children. When families lost their apartments in the bombings, they were taken in by those who still had a home.

House committees were formed by people in the courtyards who organized themselves into leadership groups to help the tenants in their building. There was a house committee in almost every apartment building which met regularly to discuss problems or issues and ways to solve them.

One important job of the house committee was to collect food from families in the building and give the food to starving families. A person carrying a bucket went to each apartment and collected food and clothing from those who were able to give whatever they could spare.

There were over 1,000 house committees throughout the Warsaw Ghetto. In addition to collecting food for the needy, the house committees organized different activities for the people in their buildings. "Children's corners" provided hot meals and lessons for young children. Older children and teenagers often volunteered and set up "youth committees" to help care for the children.

"Women's Circles" met together to run soup kitchens and set up sewing clubs to provide clothing for children and poorer families. Women played a large role in the relief efforts and took over the leadership of many house committees.

Emanuel entered the courtyard of 24 Leszno Street and made his way to the meeting. It had become very difficult to organize meetings of more than one house committee, but today all of the house committees on Leszno Street were meeting together.

"Emanuel, my friend, you made it! I was getting worried," said Moshe, the head of one of the house committees. "Attention everyone, let's get started," Moshe said loudly.

Emanuel strode to the front of the room and looked over the large group that had gathered. He saw men and women who were tired, worried, and probably hungry. He saw people who were angry about what was happening to their families and communities, and probably also afraid of what might lie ahead. He also saw strong men and women who were dedicated to a job that many others did not want to do. They were willing to step up and lead when others were not.

"It's good to see you all here," Emanuel greeted them. "We are all here for the same reasons. There are many problems we need to discuss, but we can only get to a few of those today. Let's start with the big problem of electricity. As you all know, electricity is going off for hours throughout the ghetto." The group nodded and began raising their hands to speak.

"The Germans make us pay for electricity," said one man.

"Last week the electricity was off from 7:00 am until 10:00 pm," shouted another.

The woman next to him agreed and said, "The lack of light is ruining almost all community activities. We are almost helpless without it!" she exclaimed.

Emanuel listened and nodded. "You are all exactly right. Unfortunately, with the German policy of collective responsibility, if one family or building does not pay their electric bill, the electricity for the whole building or street could be turned off. That's why it is so important to continue to demand that all tenants contribute and do their share."

As the meeting continued, the group discussed not only electricity, but other issues such as the food supply, helping the families of those who had to report for forced labor, soup kitchens, and stopping the spread of typhus. Typhus was a highly contagious disease caused by lice and over-crowded, unsanitary conditions.

The meeting ended with a plan for raising money to help pay the electric bills on Leszno Street. The following week, a group of actors and actresses would come to the courtyard of 24 Leszno Street before curfew. They would perform a concert and then stay overnight. Tenants of the buildings would pay a few zlotys (Polish money) to attend the courtyard theater. Tables would also be set up where people could play cards and gamble. The money raised would be distributed among the Leszno Street house committees to help pay electric bills and provide meals for street children at the soup kitchens.

As Emanuel left the meeting and headed home, he was weary and exhausted, but he also felt a sense of pride. In spite of brutal German policies and all of the problems in the ghetto, the house committees were standing strong and trying to provide order and stability.

The Jews in the Warsaw Ghetto were determined to prove they could rally together, make decisions for themselves, and survive.

Jews in the Warsaw Ghetto awaiting their turn in the soup kitchen, 1941. United States Holocaust Memorial Museum.

SEVEN

June 1941
Warsaw Ghetto

A secret group of writers? As she left the meeting at Emanuel Ringelblum's apartment, Rachel tried to settle the thoughts racing through her head. She was used to talking with Emanuel about the soup kitchens or other issues in the ghetto, but this was something entirely new. Emanuel wouldn't give her too many details, except to say that the group had been actively writing and collecting documents on life in the ghetto for several months. Members of the group worked on their own, not knowing who the other members were. The project required total secrecy.

It would be hard work. It would also be dangerous, but when Emanuel asked Rachel to join and write for the Oyneg Shabes, she did not hesitate. Her topic would be the soup kitchen she ran on 40 Leszno Street.

As she hurried back to the soup kitchen and turned at the corner of Leszno Street, Rachel saw the long line of people waiting anxiously for their daily bowl of soup. For many people in the ghetto, this bowl of soup was their only meal for the day. The food ration for Jews was starvation level. The German rule was that Germans received 2,613 calories per day. Poles received 699 calories per day, and Jews received 184 calories. Often, one loaf of bread was supposed to last one family for one week. When the bread ran out in two or three days, the family had to rely on the soup kitchen for food. People also began to sell clothing and personal items for money to buy food.

By the summer of 1941, the public soup kitchen at 40 Leszno Street was serving 2,000 "customers" every day. The soup kitchens were also able to bring in smuggled food, which could bring the daily calorie count up to 500 for Jews. This was still not enough to stay alive for more than a few months unless more food could be found.

Each person or family who came to the soup kitchen followed the same routine. First, they had to use their identity card to get a certificate from their specific house committee. The certificate then had to be taken to the Jewish Self-Help office for a voucher. The voucher was used to register at the soup kitchen, where the people were given tickets for free soup. One ticket equaled one bowl of soup. There were over 100 soup kitchens in the Warsaw Ghetto. These kitchens were fighting on the front lines in the desperate war against hunger.

As Rachel entered the soup kitchen, she was met by bustling workers, steaming pots, and the sounds of many quiet conversations. She took the time to stop and talk with families seated at the tables.

"How are you, Sonia? How is your little one?"

"Jacob, you look like you are feeling a little better today."

Each family had its own history. As she moved through the tables to take up tickets from those waiting to be seated, they discussed the latest news or soup recipes.

"Mr. Abrams, I see you brought your own bowl again," Rachel said with a smile. Mr. Abrams nodded, shifted his walking cane to his other hand, and held up his arm. A tin can hung from his wrist on a long piece of string. Rachel knew there were times when Mr. Abrams was unable to walk to the Jewish Self-Help office to get a voucher for a ticket. As she talked, Rachel winked quickly at one of the kitchen workers, who then served Mr. Abrams his soup without a ticket.

After a long workday in the soup kitchen, Rachel finally sat down at the desk in her small apartment at 66 Leszno Street, 12 doors down from the soup kitchen. A glance at the clock showed that it was almost midnight. A blank notebook lay open in front of her. Since the start of the war and the bombing of Warsaw, Rachel had been unable to write. She couldn't find the words to express the pain, heartache, and devastation that she had witnessed. But now it was time. She would join Emanuel and the others and write for the Oyneg Shabes. She would write about the soup kitchen at 40 Leszno Street.

Wave after wave of images flowed through her mind, but how could she write about the soup kitchen without beginning with Halina? Halina Geldman was the quiet boss of the soup kitchen. Born and raised in Warsaw, Halina knew how to run a kitchen. She organized an office, arranged shelves and storage areas, and made sure workers had hooks on which to hang their aprons. She organized a small medicine cabinet and a sewing kit with needles, thread, and thimbles.

Rachel picked up a pen and began to write. She wrote about the pots, pans, sights, smells, cooks, and workers. But behind all of this was Halina. She wrote about the blue striped aprons which Halina made for the two of them and how she often placed the apron around Rachel's neck with a reassuring smile. She wrote about Halina's kindness and compassion for others and how she made the kitchen like a home. But mostly she wrote about how Halina's friendship gave her strength.

Two children beg for food on the streets of the Warsaw Ghetto. United States Holocaust Memorial Museum.

EIGHT

December 1941
Warsaw Ghetto

The day was grey and windy. Heavy rain mixed with snow was falling. Israel shivered and crammed his hands further into his thin overcoat to try and get warmer. He and two other teachers waited in the soup kitchen to pick up the breakfast for the young children who came to their playroom and school.

The kitchen workers filled the buckets with steaming oats, and Israel and the teachers started their long walk through the rain and snow to the school. They walked slowly through the mud and crowded streets carrying the heavy buckets, making sure that none of the oats spilled over.

In September 1941, the Germans had permitted elementary schools to be opened in the Warsaw Ghetto. Secondary schools were forbidden. Thousands of young children were organized into three grades. Teachers worked very hard to create a welcoming and cheerful atmosphere for children who were hungry, cold, and often sick. Many children had no warm clothes or shoes, but they came to school every day because school was the brightest spot in their day. At school, children knew they would read stories, draw pictures, and maybe even have a few toys to play with. They also knew they would be fed. Children were eager to play and learn, but food was the most important need of every day.

As Israel and the teachers entered the playroom, the children gathered immediately around the magical hot food. "What do we always do before we eat," one teacher asked?

"Wash our hands, the children yelled, as they held up their clean hands.

The children sat down at the tables with their ragtag collection of bowls, cups, pans, and even flowerpots, for their meal. To practice good manners, the children knew that they must say, "good morning" and "thank you" as the steaming oatmeal was set before them. They always finished every bite. As the children ate, Israel counted... 66 children today. Most of them came from burned out apartments or were refugees from smaller towns and villages outside Warsaw. Many of them were orphans.

As he finished the count for the day's records, Israel noticed a small boy of six or seven sitting quietly. Israel knew he was an orphan and was on his own in the ghetto. He was one of the many who begged daily on the streets and probably stole whatever he could find to eat.

"Come here, Nathan. How are you today?" Israel asked. As Nathan slowly began to smile, Israel picked him up into his lap. "Now that you have finished eating, let me check your feet."

Israel pulled the freezing wet rags off Nathan's feet,

rubbed the boy's icy feet to warm them, and wrapped them in clean, dry rags. "Does that feel better," Israel asked?

"Yes, thank you," Nathan said shyly. Across the room, the teachers called the children to them. The children began to gather around their teachers.

"See you tomorrow," Israel said. "Now run over and listen to the story."

As Israel prepared to leave, the children listened to a story about the squirrels and rabbits in winter. Israel smiled. For a few hours at least, these children could forget the overcrowded rooms, starvation, and filth of the Warsaw Ghetto. Now it was time to move on to the next part of his day – the older children and the youth.

In Poland, the Nazi goal was to train workers and farmers. Only elementary and trade schools were allowed. Secondary schools and college-level classes were outlawed. As a result, secret classes began to spring up throughout the ghetto. Study-groups were formed by teachers for students from their former schools. Most study-groups were made up of 6 to 20 students and one teacher.

It was difficult to find safe places to meet. Textbooks, tables, paper, and other supplies were scarce. In spite of these challenges, the number of students and teachers meeting together continued to grow. There were several hundred of these secret study-groups in the Warsaw Ghetto.

Israel waited in the back room of a friend's apartment, where his own study-group was meeting this week. The group would change locations again soon to avoid raising the suspicions of the Nazi guards. Israel heard the secret knock and quietly opened the door. There stood David and Nahum. They entered quickly as the door shut behind them. Other students would be coming soon. The boys grinned as they pulled books from under their coats. Walking through the crowded ghetto streets, it was important not to draw attention to oneself. David and Nahum had been helping Israel in the soup kitchen for several months, and they loved being part of his study-group. After all, Mr. Lichtenstein had always been their favorite teacher.

Students and teachers alike faced dangers in resisting and defying the German rules against education. But that is exactly what it was – resistance. Israel, David, Nahum, and so many other teachers and students were determined to continue their studies. They proudly realized that learning was one thing the Nazis would never be able to take away from them.

Paper candy wrapper - a saccharine candy produced in the Warsaw Ghetto from the Wiktoria Sweets Factories; found in Ringelblum Archive. Courtesy of the Jewish Historical Institute in Warsaw, Poland.

NINE

December 1941
Warsaw Ghetto

The Great Synagogue on Tlomackie Street was the symbol of Jewish Warsaw. The Main Judaic Library, which was home to over 30,000 books, was located next door. Before the war began, scholars, rabbis, and students roamed the halls of the massive library, studying and debating. After the Germans occupied Warsaw, they looted the library and stole thousands of books. The synagogue and library were now inside the ghetto walls. The library was also the headquarters of the Jewish Self-Help Organization (ZSS), which the Nazis allowed to stay in operation. Little did they know that the ZSS was also involved in leading underground resistance activity.

On his way to the Jewish Self-Help office, Emanuel stood in the Main Judaic Library and looked sadly at the empty shelves. He was sad, but also angry.

"The Nazis can steal as many important books as they want," Emanuel thought to himself. "They will not erase Jewish history by stealing books. And they will not erase the story of life in the ghetto. The secret writings in our hidden archive will remain to tell our story."

A blast of cold air and a slamming door jolted Emanuel from his thoughts. His close friend, Hersh Wasser, entered the library. It was Saturday and time for their weekly Oyneg Shabes meeting.

Emanuel and Hersh both worked for the Jewish Self-Help Organization. But they were also both involved in the secret work of the Oyneg Shabes. The inner circle, or executive committee, of the Oyneg Shabes met every Saturday at the Jewish Self-Help office, which was a perfect cover for their activities. Meeting on Saturday did not look suspicious because Saturday is the Jewish Sabbath.

Since November 1940, Emanuel had worked slowly and steadily to organize a group of writers who would contribute to the secret archive. To get an accurate picture of life in the ghetto, Emanuel asked different types of people to write essays or reports. There were Jewish leaders, wealthy businessmen, poor workers, rabbis, journalists, teachers, and   refugees. There were elderly people and children, men and women. None of the writers knew the identity of other writers. The inhabitants of the ghetto did not know the archive existed.

The executive committee of the Oyneg Shabes consisted of approximately ten people. They   decided what types of documents to include in the archive. They also visited the many writers to encourage them to meet deadlines. They raised money to buy paper, notebooks, and writing supplies. They also did what they could to keep writers from starving by providing them with a little extra food and free soup at Rachel's soup kitchen.

There was also a group of volunteers who worked at

typing or hand-copying the original essay and reports. Two or three copies were often made in case the original was lost or destroyed. In all, approximately 50-60 people were involved in some way with the Oyneg Shabes archive. The only people who knew the identities of everyone involved were Emanuel and the members of the executive committee.

There was still one more group working for the Oyneg Shabes. A secret group made up of Israel Lichtenstein, David Graber, and Nahum Grzywacz was responsible for storing and hiding the archive. They were the only ones who knew where the materials were hidden. Only Emanuel and Hersh knew the identity of these three.

This Saturday, as Emanuel and the executive committee gathered in the cold, dim office at the library, brilliant white snow floated past the windows and settled on the mud and filth on Tlomackie Street. The main item on this week's agenda was organizing a public writing contest. The committee members outlined the rules and important details. "To summarize," Emanuel said, "the competition will be for young people from 15-20 years of age. The topic for the papers will focus on the changes in the lives of young people since the German occupation. The papers should include facts and personal examples, and be 25 to 30 pages in length. The deadline for entries is in four weeks. The prizes will be 200 zlotys for first place, 100 zlotys for second place, and 50 zlotys for third place."

"Don't forget the questionnaire," one member said.

"Yes," Emanuel said. "Each entrant will also fill out the questionnaire we created."

Before ending the meeting, Emanuel asked Hersh to update the committee on the archive's inventory. Hersh opened a notebook and began to read: "The Oyneg Shabbat archive currently has collected reports, essays, questionnaires, underground newspapers, drawings, candy wrappers, ration cards, tram tickets, theater posters, photographs, reports from doctors and nurses, jokes, poems, songs, postcards, and children's essays. We continue to add to this list every day," Hersh said quietly.

In that moment of silence in the nearly empty library, Emanuel, Hersh, and the executive committee understood the gravity of their mission. Regardless of what happened, they would risk their lives to document and keep a record of Nazi crimes against the Jews in the Warsaw Ghetto and throughout Poland. This story would be told, firsthand, from the Jewish point of view.

Children on the street in the Warsaw Ghetto, 1941. United States Holocaust Memorial Museum.

TEN

March 1942
Warsaw Ghetto

Rachel tightened her coat around her and wrapped a tattered scarf around her neck as she left the soup kitchen. The sun shone clear and bright and took a small edge off the biting cold. It was March... winter was almost over.

She walked quickly as she thought of all the errands she needed to do before returning to the soup kitchen. The crowds and masses of people on the streets made it very hard to get anywhere, and many streets were blocked off or ended suddenly. The streets in the ghetto were like a maze. Even the smallest errand could take hours.

As Rachel bumped, jostled, and hurried her way through the teeming crowds, her mind began to register the sights and sounds of the ghetto like snapshots from a camera. The sea of white armbands in the crowd. Peddlers selling armbands. Stores and stalls of people selling books, tablecloths, trousers, shoes, and the last of their possessions. Long lines of shivering people waiting to buy food. Gates, walls, and barbed wire. Tiny, dirty children begging on the sidewalks. An old woman digging through garbage. A man playing a violin and beggars dancing to earn a zloty or two. Horse-drawn wagons. Rickshaws. German soldiers laughing as they forced men and women to dance together. Women selling vegetables. Orphaned children clinging to each other for warmth...it was always the children that brought tears to her eyes.

After making several stops to check on supplies for the soup kitchen, Rachel delivered some bread to one of the workers who had typhus. Because of the overcrowding in the ghetto, typhus was spreading fast and was a threat to everyone. It was spreading especially fast among workers in soup kitchens because of their constant contact with large groups of people every day. Rachel and other kitchen organizers and workers knew that getting typhus was very likely, but they were determined to keep the soup kitchens up and running.

Rachel's last stop was to visit and check on her friend, Basia, who ran a children's library at 67 Leszno Street. Before the war, Basia Berman had been a librarian in the Warsaw public library. She continued to be a librarian, in secret, in the Warsaw Ghetto. Basia searched for children's books throughout the ghetto to create a welcoming place where children could nourish their minds. Jews were banned from using public libraries and even from creating their own lending libraries, so Basia did her work in secret.

The two rooms were filled with colorful drawings, toys, dolls, and picture books so that it would look like a gathering place for children, rather than a library. The hidden treasure was the books. More than 700 children regularly came to the children's library.

Basia delivered books to children who could not come

to the library. She regularly carried books in a briefcase to the poorest children in the refugee centers who had no shoes or boots or warm clothing. She took books to children whose apartment buildings or refugee centers were under quarantine because of typhus, and she organized readings for them. In freezing, unheated rooms, children huddled together under blankets to listen to stories about magical adventures and faraway places. Basia and her traveling library brought small moments of hope to many children in despair.

"Rachel, come in, come in," said Basia with a smile when her friend knocked on the door.

"I can't stay long, but I brought a few things for your little ones," Rachel said. "You may be able to use this doll I found, and I know you will want these two books I came across."

As the books exchanged hands, the women rose, embraced, and gave each other a knowing look. They both knew they were fighting a fierce battle to nourish those who needed them. One nourished the body, while the other nourished the soul.

After returning to the soup kitchen and closing up for the night, Rachel arrived back at her apartment. As weary as she was from the long day, she knew she needed to write. As her mind flowed over the events of the day, she wrote about the men and women she knew who worked in box factories and ink factories. In an economy where a loaf of bread cost 24 zlotys, they earned six zlotys and a bowl of soup for a day's work.

She wrote about the children who crawled through holes in the ghetto walls to smuggle potatoes. She wrote about the father who sold his shoes to buy food for his children who had typhus. She wrote about thieves and beggars. She wrote about the longing for fresh air and trees. She wrote about fear and hunger. But she also wrote about hope. She wrote about small acts of resistance she saw every single day. She wrote about children reading. She wrote about Basia.

ELEVEN

May 1942
Warsaw Ghetto

Nahum's mother, Chaya, sectioned off the loaf of bread very carefully every morning. One small slice each for Nahum and eight-year-old Samuel. One small slice each for herself and Benjamin before they left for work at the brushmaker's factory.

Different types of workshops and factories were set up by the Germans in the ghetto. Jewish men and women worked long hours at sewing, carpentry, brush-making, shoe-making, and other workshops. The Germans sold these products to make a profit. The Jewish workers earned a bowl of watery soup and slice of bread. As hard and exhausting as this was, the workers considered themselves fortunate to have a job in one of these factories. This meant the Germans considered them to be "essential workers" and were important to the war effort.

A few blocks away in the Grabers' apartment, David watched as his parents ate their small portion of bread and got ready for work. Henryk worked in a carpentry

Photograph found in Ringelblum Archive. Courtesy of the Jewish Historical Institute in Warsaw, Poland.

workshop, while Leah worked at a sewing factory which made German uniforms. David knew his parents took smaller pieces of bread for themselves so they could give more to David and Abigail.

While their parents were at work, David and Nahum often had to watch after their younger siblings. The teenage boys were not exactly happy about having to babysit, but it was a necessity. They also had another job to do. Almost every day, David, Abigail, Nahum, and Samuel walked the crowded ghetto streets looking for rags and pieces of old clothing. Even the smallest scrap of cloth could be used. They also looked for potato peelings, which were considered valuable.

By now, everyone in the ghetto knew that in order to survive, they would have to break German laws. Official German rations were not enough to keep people from starving to death. Underground businesses were everywhere; they provided families with money to pay for smuggled food. Almost 90 percent of the food Jews ate in the ghetto came from smuggling.

During the day, Nahum and David's parents worked at jobs that were considered "legal" by the German authorities. But in their homes at night, both families took part in "illegal" side-jobs to try and make money to buy more food.

On their way home after their daily scavenging, David and Nahum passed by several small plots of ground with signs that said, "Do Not Walk on the Grass." Small vegetable gardens struggled to grow in spite of often being trampled by the crowds. These vegetable plots and others throughout the ghetto were grown by a group called Toporol. David and Nahum, along with hundreds of other young people, learned how to grow vegetables at classes sponsored by Toporol. In addition to planting seeds in any fields and empty spaces in the ghetto, people tried growing potatoes, onions, carrots, and beets on the sites of gutted houses that had been destroyed in the bombings and on rooftops of apartment buildings. Families also tried growing vegetables on their tiny apartment balconies.

In their homes at night, David's and Nahum's families took part in illegal businesses to make a little money for food. Weary from working for more than 12 hours at the factory, Leah sorted through the rags and scraps of cloth that David and Abigail found during the day. The family then set to work, cutting and shredding the pieces of cloth into threads and thin strips that Leah then weaved and sewed into socks. Socks were in high demand and could be sold or traded for food.

Nahum's family cut up and ground dry potato peelings into powder. The potato powder was mixed with flour to make bread, which could be sold or traded for more food. Hunger was constant; obtaining more food was an obsession in the ghetto.

TWELVE

June 1942
Warsaw Ghetto

Israel walked quickly down the steps to the basement of the Borochov School at 68 Nowolipki Street. David and Nahum were already there. The teacher and his former students met regularly at what was now the secret hideout for the documents being collected for the Oyneg Shabes archive.

Israel was coming from a quick meeting with Hersh Wasser, who passed along material to take to the hiding place. "I have a few more to add," Israel said as he pulled wrapped documents from underneath his shirt.

Before adding them to the collection, the three sat down to look over the newest arrivals. They reviewed and discussed the variety of photographs, announcements, and essays that had been submitted. "David, look at this drawing in this underground newspaper," Nahum exclaimed, as he unrolled it. His friend didn't respond.

"David," Nahum said again.

"Sorry," David said. "I was reading this invitation to a

children's program at Dr. Korczak's orphanage."

"Ah, yes," Israel said with a smile. "That's today. Dr. Ringelblum and I are both going. In fact, I need to leave now. See you again soon at our usual time," Israel said as he gave each boy a quick smile and pat on the back. David and Nahum nodded and smiled at their teacher as they turned to pack away the documents for the archive.

On the long walk to meet Emanuel, Israel's thoughts turned to Janusz Korczak, the director of one of the largest children's orphanages in the ghetto. Before the war started, Korczak was a well-known doctor, author of children's books, and headmaster of an orphanage. After the ghetto was formed, Korczak and his assistant, Stefania Wilczynska, cared for almost 200 orphans, most of them street children. In the midst of the hardships of the ghetto, Korczak and Stefania provided the children with daily lessons, art, and opportunities to put on plays and recitals. Invitations to these performances were sent out and were very popular in the ghetto.

As the afternoon turned to dusk, Israel saw several small children scrambling back into the ghetto through holes in the walls. These were the ghetto's smallest money makers... they were smuggling. Adult smugglers often used and paid street children to smuggle items out of and back into the ghetto. As sad as it was, most ghetto inhabitants knew that life or death in the ghetto depended on smuggling.

Israel and Emanuel met outside the orphanage at 16 Sienna Street and entered together. They were greeted warmly and welcomed by Dr. Korczak, who was both a friend and a hero to the two men. "Israel, Emanuel, I'm so glad you made it. Thank you for coming. You are going to love today's production."

"We always do, Janusz," said Israel as he clasped his friend's hand. "Your children are such light and hope in this darkness."

As the children sang songs and recited poems and fables, both Israel and Emanuel were lost in thought. They thought of their own children. Surely such sweetness, innocence, and strength would endure.

Group portrait of orphans on the grounds of the Korczak Orphanage. United States Holocaust Memorial Museum.

Photograph found in Ringelblum Archive. Courtesy of the Jewish Historical Institute in Warsaw, Poland.

THIRTEEN

July 1942
Warsaw Ghetto

Smuggling continued in spite of German threats. It was done at exit points, through underground tunnels, through sewers, through holes in houses bordering the Aryan side, and across the walls. At certain places, ladders were thrown over the wall, and smugglers went back and forth all night.

The danger was extreme. Any Jew caught leaving the ghetto without a pass would receive the death penalty. Some days and nights, smugglers were caught and beaten or shot dead by German guards. But the smuggling continued because it was the salvation of the starving ghetto.

Bread cost a fortune, so people tried to sell potatoes and vegetables. Coal was nowhere to be found. A pot of hot water cost more than anyone could afford. Hunger grew. Bread-snatching was common. There were houses and apartments where everything had been sold – even the pillow cases and sheets. Basketfuls of books were being sold for cheap on the streets. English books were very popular, since so many were planning on leaving Poland after the war.

Rumors were everywhere. Reports came in from different cities and ghettos. There were reports of Jews being deported and sent away to places called Sobibor, Belzec, Chelmno, and Treblinka. The reports said that when people were sent to these places, they were never heard from again.

"This can't be true. These are only rumors," most people in the ghetto thought. This was just foolish talk that couldn't be believed. Besides, many Jews in the ghetto worked at German factories. The Warsaw Ghetto was hard at work for the Germans, and Jews were essential workers. Surely the Germans needed their labor for the war effort.

There were other rumors, too. Underground newspapers in the ghetto reported that the Russians were pushing the Germans back. There was a new saying on the street: "Jews, have no fear! Poles, rejoice! Germans, go packing!"

People became a little more optimistic and began to believe that the war would be over in a few months. Illegal radio broadcasts, listened to in secret on hidden radios, predicted more Allied victories and more German defeats. The Jews in the ghetto placed their hope in the advancing Allies and vowed to wait it out. All of this misery would end soon and life would return to normal.

New reports came in about old people and children being sent away. Wagons full of children under ten and older people over 60 disappeared from the ghettos. Jews who couldn't work were no longer useful.

An assembly point (the Umschlagplatz) in the Warsaw Ghetto for Jews rounded up for deportation. Warsaw, Poland, 1942–43. Yad Vashem Photo Archives.

On July 22, 1942 German notices were posted throughout the Warsaw Ghetto, stating that only Jews who worked in German factories and had work permits would remain in the ghetto. All others, regardless of their age, would be deported "to the East." The news spread

like lightning through the ghetto and panic spread as people tried to obtain work permits for their children and elderly relatives.

FOURTEEN

July 1942
Warsaw Ghetto

It was a Wednesday. July 22, 1942, began what was known as the Great Deportation in the Warsaw Ghetto. The German guards methodically sectioned off streets or blocks of the ghetto. Jews who lived on these blocks were forced out of their homes or places of work onto the street. Then, with bundles and packs on their backs, they were marched under guard to the Umschlagplatz, or assembly point, where they were forced to wait. As soon as one block was cleared, German guards would move to the next block and repeat the process. When the Umschlagplatz was filled with 4,000 to 5,000 people, Jews were forced to board trains made up of cattle cars. When they asked where they were going, they were told they were being sent "to the East to work." Everyone in the ghetto who did not have a work permit was now in danger of being rounded up and deported.

Along with factory workers, the members of the Jewish Council, Jewish Police, and Aleynhilf were not in danger of being deported. Because Emanuel was a leader of the Aleynhilf, the self-help society in the ghetto, he was able to move throughout the ghetto and try to help others who did not have work permits. From the first day of the Great Deportation, Emanuel prepared and gave out hundreds of Aleynhilf work certificates. In spite of the danger, Emanuel went daily to the Umschlagplatz to take work certificates to the trapped Jews. Within one week, the Germans no longer accepted these certificates.

Like other members of the Oyneg Shabes, Emanuel had to protect himself, his wife, and son by finding a place in a German workshop. He hid with his family at the carpentry workshop on 59 Nowolipki Street.

Israel hid with his wife, child, and other families in the cellar at 68 Nowolipki Street. David and Nahum also hid at 68 Nowlipki Street; they were separated from their families because it was too dangerous to try to make it back home.

On the first day of the roundups, Rachel continued to work at the soup kitchen on Leszno Street. In spite of the panic in the streets, people poured into the kitchen by the hundreds. As they sat at the tables, the kitchen staff served their soup and even gave out second helpings. As she hid in her apartment later that night, Rachel wrote, "They came in like a storm...the fear didn't lessen their hunger."

Emanuel spread the word that there would be an urgent meeting of the Oyneg Shabes on July 26. Some members of the Oyneg Shabes had already been rounded up and deported. Exhausted by fear and worry, the remaining members discussed their next steps. At the end of this sad meeting, Emanuel said quietly, "We are in agreement. We keep writing and collecting. If none of us survive, preparations must be made for the archive to be sent to America. But right now, what we have collected and hidden must be buried. It is time."

"Yes," Hersh said. "We will go out and encourage people to finish their writings. Then we will collect everything. I will gather what we have now and take it to the hiding place."

Emanuel knew that once the documents went with Hersh, the archive was out of his hands. The only person on the committee who knew the location of the hideout was Hersh Wasser. Meanwhile, at 68 Nowolipki Street, Israel, David, and Nahum waited for the signal to bury the archive.

*Three of the ten metal boxes in which portions of the Ringel-
blum Oyneg Shabes archives were hidden and buried in the
Warsaw Ghetto. The boxes are currently in the possession of
the Jewish Historical Institute in Warsaw, Poland. United
States Holocaust Memorial Museum.*

FIFTEEN

July 22 – August 3, 1942
Warsaw Ghetto

The Great Deportation continued throughout late July and into August. Every day, thousands of Jews were rounded up and taken to the trains. Every day, SS guards and Jewish Police blockaded streets, searched buildings, and checked documents. Every day, 5,000 to 6,000 Jews were marched to the Umschlagplatz, loaded onto trains, and "resettled" or "sent to the East."

During blockades and round-ups, Jews stayed off the streets. It was only when the manhunts slowed or stopped for the day that people appeared on the ghetto streets again.

The leaders of the Oyneg Shabes knew there was no time to lose. Emanuel and Hersh hurried to collect as many documents from as many writers as they could reach. The documents accumulated at the hideout on 68 Nowolipki Street, where Israel, David, and Nahum waited. A lantern and a few candles cast circles of light in the darkness of the cellar. Israel, David, and Nahum sorted through the bundles and piles of documents that Hersh continued to deliver to the hideout.

"Look at these pictures of smugglers," David said, as he sat down with the photographs. The three of them often stayed up late into the night talking about all they were seeing and reading. They read, talked, packed documents, and waited.

On the sixth day of the round-ups, Rachel cautiously left her apartment to meet Hersh. Earlier that morning, she had collected her essays on the soup kitchen, her outlines, and her unfinished writings. Sitting at her desk, Rachel tore out pages from her journal that described the events of the week before the Great Deportation. So many essays and descriptions were not finished, but she had to turn them over now. There might not be another chance. Hersh and Rachel met quickly in a doorway on Leszno Street.

"This is the last of what I have," Rachel said as she handed the packet to Hersh. There was not time to say much else as they clasped each other's hands, wishing each other safety and luck.

August 2, 1942

Hersh delivered a message to Israel. It contained one word: "Legend". This was the code word meaning "bury the archive." Israel, David, and Nahum immediately began to pack all of the documents into ten metal boxes. They packed each box carefully; folding posters, newspapers, and drawings. They arranged photographs, journals, and essays.

When each box was packed, it was closed, sealed, and tied tightly with pieces of twine. Holes had already been dug beneath the foundation of 68 Nowolipki Street. The boxes would be buried here.

August 3, 1942

Nine boxes were under the foundation of the cellar, waiting to be buried. The tenth and final box was almost ready. They worked against time, because no one knew when the Germans might suddenly appear. Israel, David, and Nahum sat down to write their final messages.

Israel wrote:

...So with all the energy and enthusiasm I had, I threw myself into collecting as much material as I could for the archive. They told me that I would be the guardian of the treasure. I hid all the materials. I hid them well! May the day come when someone will find them...I do not ask for any thanks, for any memorial, for any praise...I only wish to be remembered...I wish my wife to be remembered, Gele Sekstein. I wish my little daughter to be remembered. Margalit is 20 months old today...

David wrote:

We have to hurry. We don't know what the next moment will bring. Yesterday we worked until late into the night...I want future generations to know we lived through our sufferings and our pain. They should know that during such days of disaster, there were those who had the courage to carry through this kind of task...just look at our devotion and energy as we dug holes for the containers...We have fulfilled our responsibility...We all realized that we were working for history, and that this was more important than individual lives...

Neighboring street besieged. We are all feverish. Mood tense, we prepare for worst. We hurry. Probably soon we will do our last burying. Comrade Lichtenstein nervous. Grzywacz somewhat afraid. Myself indifferent. In my subconscious, a feeling I shall get out of all trouble. Good day. We must only manage to bury the boxes. Yes, even now we don't forget it. At work until the last moment.

As Nahum wrote, he heard that the Germans had surrounded his family's building.

Right now, even as I am writing, I can hear the terrible sound of shooting coming from outside. If there's any one thing I am proud of, it's that in the very worst of the terror, I helped bury the treasure...I hid these documents so that you might know about the suffering and the killing that marked the Nazi tyranny. I am going to run to my parents and see if they are all right. I don't know what's going to happen to me. Remember, my name is Nahum Grzywacz.

Israel, David, and Nahum added their writings to the last box. It was carefully sealed and buried with the others. They had completed their mission. If the three of them did not survive, only Hersh would know where to find the archive.

Train station near the Treblinka killing center. This photo was found in an album belonging to camp commandant Kurt Franz. Poland, 1942-1943. United States Holocaust Memorial Museum.

SIXTEEN

September 1942
Warsaw Ghetto

In the final days of the Great Deportation, the Germans blockaded four streets in the ghetto and forced all Jews remaining in the ghetto to report there. It was called "the Cauldron." Work documents no longer mattered. During the next week, Jews had to appear before SS guards, who either gave them work numbers or sent them to the Umschlagplatz. During this week, more than 100,000 Jews were forced onto trains and "sent to the East."

The remaining members of the Oyneg Shabes knew it was time to go into hiding. Emanuel, Israel, Hersh, and their families hid in a concealed classroom at the former school on 68 Nowolipki Street. Emanuel and Israel continued to work and hide documents in the cellar at 68 Nowolipki.

The soup kitchen at 40 Leszno Street was turned into a kitchen to feed Jewish workers at a German workshop. Rachel and her co-workers were now in danger of being deported. Rachel went at dawn to say goodbye to her co-workers at the soup kitchen and then went into hiding with ten other people in a tiny coal cellar in her apartment building at 66 Leszno Street. The entrance to the cellar was hidden under a rug, table, and chairs.

When this horrible phase of the Great Deportation ended, those who were in hiding slowly began to come back out. The German blockades ended for a while. The ghetto was now one big labor camp.

Emanuel and Israel worked at a carpentry workshop. Rachel worked at a honey factory, but she was also given another assignment. Emanuel asked Rachel to write about her interviews with a man who escaped from a place called Treblinka. He supplied her with extra paper and gas lamps for light, so that she could finish as quickly as possible. Rumors about Treblinka had already reached the ghetto months before. Where was it? Why were so many Jews being sent there? Why did their families never hear from them again? After many hours of interviewing and writing, Rachel found the answers to these questions.

Treblinka was a small village located 50 miles away from Warsaw. A major railroad line went through this area and there was a railroad station near the village. In July 1942, Nazi officials completed the construction of the death camp known as Treblinka, which was to be a killing center for Jews. There were ten gas chambers located there.

Treblinka was hidden in a heavily wooded area. It was surrounded by barbed wire and guard towers. Branches were woven into the barbed wire and trees were planted around the fences so that no one could see into the camp from the outside. Incoming trains of about 55 cattle cars arrived daily filled with Jews from the Warsaw Ghetto.

The stories about Treblinka were no longer rumors. They were facts. There were no longer any questions about what the Nazis intended to do with the Jews in the Warsaw Ghetto.

The leaders of the Oyneg Shabes began to print and send out messages to the Jews in the ghetto telling them not to believe it when the Germans said there would be no more deportations. Treblinka was still in operation. The message was to resist the Nazis in any way possible. There was also another message: start preparing to fight.

SEVENTEEN

Fall 1942
Warsaw Ghetto

By now, everyone left in the ghetto had heard of Treblinka. Everyone had lost someone... a wife, husband, parent, child, friend. In late July, there had been hundreds of thousands of Jews in the ghetto. Of the 60,000 who now remained, there were hardly any children or elderly people. The Jews who were still in the ghetto were either "legal," which meant they had a work number and worked in one of the German workshops. Or they were "wild," which meant they did not have a work number and were in hiding.

Since September, the daily deportations had stopped. Discarded bedding, pillows, clothing, and broken furniture were scattered throughout the courtyards and streets. No one was allowed in the streets anymore. Workers and their families could not leave their workshops.

Emanuel and a few other members of the Oyneg Shabes worked in German workshops and were able to stay in contact. In spite of all of the horrible things they had seen and experienced, Emanuel encouraged them to keep writing and collecting evidence, as he did. He also had an idea that might help Jews who were left in the ghetto. Secretly, Emanuel gathered with a few trusted friends and talked about his plan.

"We may not be able to do much, but we can do something," Emanuel said. "I'm going to ask the German officials if we can start a new committee. We will have to make it sound like it will make their workshops more productive."

"That's the only way they will approve anything," someone murmured.

"That's right," Emanuel agreed, "and that's how I'll present it to them. I'll make the case that improving living conditions, caring for sick workers, and providing more food and warm clothing will make them work harder. What do you think?" Emanuel asked.

His friends agreed to help. As Emanuel wrote out the plan to present to German officials, his real goals were unwritten. The real goals were to help Jews in the ghetto stay alive, stay strong, and hold on.

The Germans agreed to Emanuel Ringelbum's plan for a new Jewish aid organization in the ghetto. Emanuel now had permission to meet regularly with workers in other shops. It was dangerous for others to be out in the streets, but Emanuel could move about freely from shop to shop. Not only was he able to stay in contact with members of the Oyneg Shabes, but he also began to witness different groups in the ghetto that were preparing to fight back.

Emanuel began to write about a new chapter in the history of the Warsaw Ghetto. He wrote about hidden radios, revolvers, rifles, stolen German uniforms, and hand grenades. He wrote about Jewish resistance.

An underground bunker, built by Jews in Warsaw in preparation for anti-Nazi resistance. United States Holocaust Memorial Museum.

EIGHTEEN

December 24, 1942
Warsaw Ghetto

"Hideouts"
by Emanuel Ringelblum

...Everybody is now making hideouts. They are being built everywhere, in all the shops in the ghetto...Craftsmen, engineers, and others earn a living from it.

...A new series of hideouts began after the selection, when life in the ghetto had quieted down somewhat. People learned not to believe the Germans.

People thus began to think of ways to protect themselves in case of danger. Some, the richer ones, began to cross over to the other side. Others began to think about hideouts. In November and December, people went about feverishly constructing hideouts. These hideouts, however, were completely different from the ones built in the summer during the 'action.' First, they had to be adapted to the cold period, and second they were set up in such a way so that people could spend entire months in them. The thinking behind the hideouts was thus: if all the Jews in Warsaw were liquidated, we would go into the hideouts and remain there until redemption came. These hideouts are constructed 1) in

basements, 2) underground, and 3) on one of the floors.
...Some hideouts are built on (above-ground) floors. They are
built in an alcove or a corner room and walled in so they are
completely unrecognizable... People cooperated with all their
neighbors and walled in all the alcoves. In a different building,
one corner room is walled in on each floor, an entrance has been
constructed through an oven, and a passageway from one floor to
another has been made using ladders that connect one room to
the next through holes hacked out of the floor. Such an impressive
hideout can take in up to 60 people...

NINETEEN

January 1943
Warsaw Ghetto

Since mid-September, there had been no deportations. The Jews who remained in the ghetto labored through the winter and waited. Were the deportations over? On January 18, 1943, that question was answered as German guards and soldiers stormed into the ghetto. Their goal was to round up and deport 8,000 more Jews.

By now, most Jews knew not to believe German promises that they were being sent to labor camps and refused to report when they received a deportation notice. When the Germans entered the ghetto, they encountered empty streets. Most Jews in the ghetto were now in hideouts and bunkers. The Germans also encountered something else. For the first time in the history of the Warsaw Ghetto, they were caught off guard by armed resistance.

The Jewish fighting groups in the ghetto were also caught off guard by the German attack. They still did not have many weapons, but they used what they had to fight back. Small fighting groups throughout the ghetto attacked German guards.

One group hid and waited on the Nazis with a stash of four revolvers, four grenades, clubs, and steel pipes. They killed two Germans and wounded several. The Germans were thrown into a state of confusion and fled the ghetto.

The Nazi Aktion lasted four days, but they did not reach their goal of rounding up 8,000 victims. They did manage to round up 6,500, but most of these were caught on the first day during the surprise attack. The German soldiers now knew that venturing into the maze of the ghetto streets and searching for hideouts could mean a fierce battle.

The resistance motivated the fighters and the ghetto population. They had fought back and the Germans retreated! News coming in from the battlefields brought reports of German defeats in North Africa and Stalingrad.

The Jews in the ghetto became more determined than ever to build hideouts and prevent future roundups. They also became more determined than ever to fight back and hold on until the war ended.

TWENTY

February–March 1943
Warsaw Ghetto

After the fighting in the ghetto in January, Emanuel knew he had to make a decision. For months, friends who had escaped the ghetto tried to persuade him to leave the ghetto, join them, and help them with underground work on the Aryan side. He had lost many friends and now knew that the only way to save his wife, Judyta, and son, Uri, was to find a hideout outside the ghetto.

Emanuel had already begun to leave the ghetto regularly to meet with a network of friends who were working with the underground resistance. It was very dangerous, but he walked out of the ghetto with groups of Jewish workers who were being marched to work sites. Once outside the ghetto, he left the workers and met with friends working for the resistance. At the end of the day, he marched back into the ghetto with the workers.

In early February, Emanuel decided that it was time to get his family out of the ghetto. Hersh was struggling with the same decision. The two friends were still able to meet secretly at their workshops where they agonized over unanswerable questions. Could they get their families out of the ghetto? Would their hideouts on the other side be safe? What would happen to the archive? If they were able to save themselves and their families, what would happen to those left behind?

Sometime in early February, Emanuel and his family escaped the ghetto and went into hiding in a large underground bunker that was built under a greenhouse on 81 Grojecka Street. The bunker contained more than 30 people.

Also sometime in early February, Emanuel gave the order to bury the second part of the archive beneath the foundation of 68 Nowolipki Street. Did Emanuel bury it himself? Did Israel receive the message and bury the archive? Did they work on it together? No one knows the answers to these questions. What is known is that the second part of the archive was buried in two large aluminum milk cans under the same cellar at 68 Nowolipki.

Some of the last documents to be placed in the milk cans were Emanuel's essays on the Oyneg Shabes Archive and accounts of the fighting that had just taken place in January. Whoever found the archive would now know that the Jews in the Warsaw Ghetto were not only resisting with words, they were fighting back with any weapon they could find.

Hersh Wasser and his wife, Bluma, also escaped the ghetto to hide on the Aryan side in February 1943. Rachel Auerbach escaped to the Aryan side in March 1943.

Before Rachel left the ghetto, she was hurrying to say goodbye to a friend when she unexpectedly saw Emanuel.

They talked quietly. "The archive is secure," he told her. It is safe from fire and water." Emanuel told her that he had given the order to bury and seal the archive, and the code word "Legend" had been sent to the Aryan side.

He did not say where the archive was buried, and Rachel knew not to ask. Rachel later wrote, "For a moment I felt transported to some future, later time when everything that we did and saw would become, for the Jews who survived,~a legend."

Even though he was in hiding on the Aryan side, Emanuel frequently returned to the ghetto to try to find ways to get other people out. He organized meetings to rescue as many Jewish children as possible. He also continued to try to rescue members of the Oyneg Shabes, scholars, writers, and actors. He made many dangerous visits back into the ghetto to try to save his close friends, including Israel, his wife Gele, and their young daughter, Margalit.

A German gun crew shells a housing block during the suppression of the Warsaw Ghetto uprising. Poland, April 19-May 16, 1943. United States Holocaust Memorial Museum..

TWENTY-ONE

April 1943
Warsaw Ghetto

Spring was slowly coming back to the ghetto. It was almost Passover, and Emanuel was back in the ghetto. He met with members of one of the fighting groups and was planning to attend a Passover service. His main focus was still on rescuing close friends.

Hersh was also back in the ghetto. He and Emanuel sent a message to Israel, who joined them at the workshop where they were staying. The friends talked until late into the night. Little did they know that as they talked, German troops surrounded the ghetto. Their goal was to round up all of the remaining Jews and deport them to Treblinka. The fighters in the ghetto anticipated more fighting and went on high alert, ready to rise up and fight.

The signal for the uprising would be when the Nazis entered the ghetto and attempted to resume the deportations. Word spread throughout the ghetto that anyone who had a weapon was to come out to fight. Anyone who did not have a weapon was to go into the hiding places and bunkers.

On April 19, the eve of Passover, the final uprising of the Warsaw Ghetto began. Just before the fighting started, Israel left the workshop and tried to make it back to his family's hideout at 68 Nowolipki Street. Emanuel never saw his friend again.

When the German soldiers streamed into the ghetto, they were met with empty, silent streets. Suddenly, Jewish fighters attacked, armed with a handful of pistols, grenades (many of them homemade), seventeen rifles, and a few automatic weapons. 750 Jewish fighters faced more than 2,000 heavily armed German troops.

As the battle raged around him, Emanuel was trapped in the ghetto and couldn't get back out to his wife and son. He was captured by the Germans in the first few hours of the battle and later sent to a labor camp called Trawniki.

On the first day of fighting, the German soldiers were stunned by the attack and retreated outside the ghetto walls. On the third day of fighting, the Nazis changed their strategy. They returned with tanks and flamethrowers and began to burn the ghetto, building by building, to force the remaining Jews out of the bunkers. The fighting continued day after day for weeks, and the ghetto was reduced to rubble. The skies of Warsaw were completely red.

Pockets of resistance fighters fought heroically from the bunkers until they were forced out by smoke and raging fires. This small group of Jewish fighters held off the mighty German army for nearly a month. The German soldiers finally overcame the Jewish fighters, and the uprising ended.

The Warsaw Ghetto Uprising became a symbol of resistance and an example for Jews in other ghettos and camps.

Rachel Auerbach. Yad Vashem Photo Archive.

TWENTY-TWO

August 1943
Warsaw Ghetto

The former Warsaw Ghetto was now in ruins. Buildings, apartments, houses, shops, and courtyards now lay in piles of brick, stone, and twisted metal. As a final blow, the Great Synagogue on Tlomackie Street, once the symbol of Jewish Warsaw, was destroyed by the Germans to symbolize their victory.

The Germans deported the remaining Jews from the ghetto to Treblinka or to forced-labor camps. Those who managed to escape the ghetto before the Uprising were still in hiding on the Aryan side. This included Rachel and Hersh. The other members of the Oyneg Shabes were either in hiding or had been deported. No one knew for sure.

It had been almost three months since anyone had heard from Emanuel. Jewish resistance workers on the Aryan side finally found out he was imprisoned at Trawniki, a forced-labor camp. Through a network of couriers and a series of bribes, they were able to sneak Emanuel out of the camp and onto a train back to Warsaw.

Meanwhile, Rachel had fake documents, a new name, and was renting a small room from a Polish woman on the Aryan side. To make money to survive, she sold socks. On the very day that Emanuel arrived back in Warsaw, Rachel happened to be delivering socks to friends who were also part of the resistance on the Aryan side and were the ones who were hiding Emanuel. They told Rachel he was there. "He's right here, in the other room?" Rachel asked excitedly. Yes, and if she was willing to wait, she could see him.

"And that's exactly what happened!" Rachel later wrote. As Rachel walked into the room, Emanuel clasped her hands. "Rachel, I am so happy you're alive. And you look just like an Aryan woman," Emanuel said with a smile. The two friends talked about many topics. They knew they didn't have long to visit. Emanuel told her about Trawniki and the horrors of the camp. "The workers there are planning to resist," he told her. He asked what she could tell him about what had been happening in Warsaw.

"We've been hearing so much news on our radios," she told him excitedly. "Mussolini has fallen. What we've been waiting on for so long is happening! I even saw an article that said, 'Without Mussolini, no Hitler' Surely the end of the war is in sight!"

Emanuel listened and became very serious. "Only with liberation," he replied, "will we really begin to realize what we have endured, and then our real pain will begin." As their meeting ended, both friends wondered if they would see each other again.

Within a few days, Emanuel returned to Judyta and Uri in the bunker on 81 Grojecka Street. For the next seven months, he remained there, writing about the Trawniki labor camp. His friends in the resistance visited him after dark to collect his writings. They told Emanuel that he could possibly be smuggled out of Poland into Hungary. He refused. He would not leave his wife and son again.

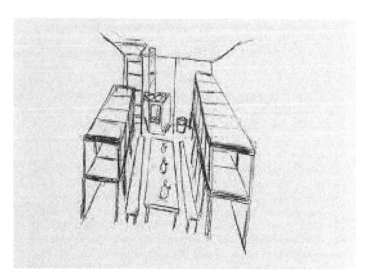

"Sketch of the bunker as seen from the inside." From *The Hiding Place*, by Orna Jagur.

TWENTY-THREE

August 1943 – March 1944
Krysia: The Bunker

The hideout where Emanuel, his family, and nearly 40 other Jews were hidden was nicknamed "Krysia". Behind the house at 81 Grojecka Street, there was a small garden full of flowers and an ivy-covered pavilion. A narrow path led through the garden to a long building covered with glass windows. The bunker was under this greenhouse. Mieczyslaw Wolski and his mother Malgorzata, lived in the house at 81 Grojecka. Wolski's sisters, mother, and 17-year-old nephew, Janusz, took care of the Jews who were hiding in the bunker.

During the daytime, Janusz stayed near the greenhouse to watch out for German soldiers, garden workers, or neighbors who might come too close. When there was danger nearby, Janusz whistled a certain song. When it was safe, he whistled another song. Yet another song was the signal for the people inside to open the flap, which led down into the bunker.

The Krysia was a long narrow rectangle, about 23 feet

long and 16 feet wide. It had two rows of double bunk beds along each wall. Between the bunk beds, there were long tables with benches on each side. A few small portable lamps sat along the tables and provided dim, flickering light.

Every Jew who hid in the bunker had to pay a fixed amount of money up front, in addition to making regular payments for food. In German-occupied Warsaw during the war, finding and paying for food was very difficult. To explain the amount of food he had to purchase to feed the Jews in the bunker, Wolski arranged for a relative to open a grocery store in his house.

It was not uncommon for people to turn in their neighbors if they suspected they were hiding Jews. The Nazis gave money, sugar, liquor, and food to anyone who turned in Jews or those hiding Jews. Anyone caught helping Jews who had fled the Warsaw Ghetto was put to death.

In the Krysia, there were daily and nightly routines. During the day, there were strict rules and there was no cooking or talking. The flap to the outside was closed. The stale air in the bunker reeked. People lay on their bunks or sat at the table. Children whispered and played. Coughs or sneezes were muffled by a pillow or blanket.

The "day" for everyone in the bunker actually started in the evening after workers and neighbors went home. Janusz brought food, carried out the garbage, and emptied the bathroom buckets. One person at a time could climb the ladder to breathe a little fresh air. The cooking was done at night and everyone shared the evening meal together.

The group tried to keep their spirits up by having small

celebrations on holidays. Wolski often visited the hideout at night and shared daily news that he heard from listening to an illegal radio. He confidently told the hidden Jews to keep hanging on and that they would survive the war. He told them the hideout was safe beyond a doubt.

Even there, in the dark, crowded, bug-infested bunker, Emanuel continued to write. Day after day, he sat in the same place at one of the long tables, and wrote about what he had seen and experienced. He also penned essays about poets, historians, actors, rabbis, writers, and teachers that he wanted to be remembered. While the bleak daily routine in the Krysia carried on around him, Emanuel's thoughts were often far away. The Germans were determined to destroy every trace of Jewish history and culture. Emanuel's mission was to preserve and save it.

Emanuel Ringelblum with his son Uri. Yad Vashem Photo Archives.

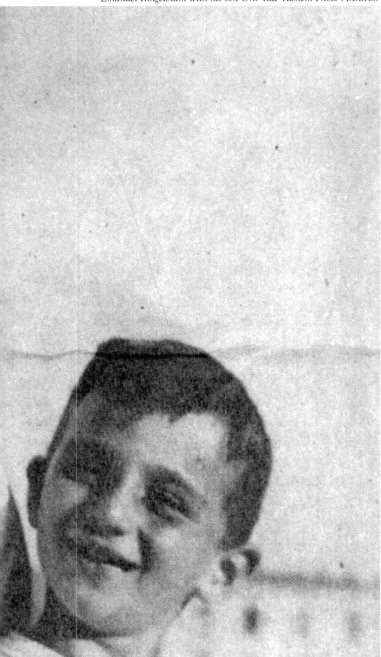

TWENTY-FOUR

March 7, 1944
The Krysia – 81 Grojecka Street
Warsaw, Poland

It was a bitterly cold day that began like almost every other day. The 38 Jews in the Krysia sat on their bunks or at the tables, mending clothing, sleeping, writing, or talking in whispers. The day was like any other day; until it wasn't. There was shouting outside. Emanuel looked up from his writing. There was yelling and banging on the walls. The Jews in the Krysia stood and looked at each other in terror. They stared at the opening to the outside. Voices screamed angrily, "Get out, Jews! Come out! Hands up!"

Emanuel pulled Uri and Judyta closer to him. "Daddy, what's happening?" Uri whispered fearfully. Nobody spoke or moved. Now there were gunshots outside.

"Come out or we will poison you all like rats," the voices yelled.

The flap that led to the outside was raised slowly, and the Jews hiding in the Krysia emerged one by one.

Mothers and their children came out first, almost blinded by the glare of sunlight they had not seen in months.

The Nazis continued to yell and fire shots into the air. Children cried. Helplessly, mothers held them close. Next, the other adults came out silently. At the end of the line was Janusz. The 38 Jews who had been in hiding together for more than seven months stood in the garden. They saw Wolski, who had been kicked and beaten, surrounded by Polish police. Wolski's mother had also been dragged out of the house.

Wolski cried out, "Yes, I hid these people, but I am the only one responsible! My mother, my sisters, and family did not know anything! Kill me but leave my family alone! They are innocent!"

Pushing them and screaming, the Gestapo men loaded all of the Jews, Wolski, and Janusz into trucks and drove away. Before leaving, the Gestapo threw grenades into the Krysia and blew it up.

The captured Jews, including Emanuel, Judyta, and Uri, were taken to Pawiak Prison, which was located in the destroyed Warsaw Ghetto. Men and women were put in separate cells. Uri was sent with his father.

One of the prisoners in Pawiak was able to visit with Emanuel. He went into Emanuel's cell. Uri was sitting on his lap. Emanuel had been badly beaten. He told the prisoner that the Gestapo had questioned him and tried to get him to tell the names of others in the Jewish underground resistance.

The prisoner hurriedly told him that other Jewish inmates wanted to try and smuggle Emanuel out of his cell and into a prison work detail. Emanuel held Uri closer. "What about my son and wife?" Emanuel asked.

The prisoner told him that smuggling Judyta and Uri out would not be possible. Emanuel said he would stay.

Within a few days, the Germans took the 38 prisoners of the Krysia to the charred remains of the Warsaw Ghetto, where they were all shot. Emanuel, Judyta, and Uri were among them. Mieczyslaw Wolski and his nephew, Janusz Wysocki, had been shot very soon after their arrest.

How did the Germans find the Krysia? Wolski and his girlfriend had an argument. Out of anger, the girlfriend told an 18-year-old friend about the hideout. Her friend then informed the Gestapo. When the Gestapo and Polish police showed up at the Wolski home on 81 Grojecka Street, they knew exactly where to look.

Clandestine photograph of the destroyed Warsaw Ghetto. United States Holocaust Memorial Museum.

TWENTY-FIVE

March 1944
Warsaw, Poland

On the streets of Warsaw, everybody was talking about the 38 Jews caught in the bunker. Rachel, still hiding in plain sight and working on the Aryan side, heard the devastating news about Emanuel's death. She later wrote, "Those of us who had been his friends and co-workers on the Aryan side were crushed by this calamity. After surviving so many close calls, he perished. And less than a year before the liberation."

On August 1, 1944 the Polish Home Army, along with citizens of Warsaw, rose up and fought bravely against their German occupiers. This was known as the Warsaw Uprising (not the same as the Warsaw Ghetto Uprising). By the end of September, the Germans had regained control and set out to destroy the whole city. Warsaw now lay completely shattered.

TWENTY-SIX

April 1946
Warsaw, Poland

After escaping from the ghetto and living on the Aryan side, Rachel continued the work of the Oyneg Shabes Archive. She wrote essays on the ghetto, her soup kitchen, the Great Deportation, and Treblinka. She became a secret courier for the Jewish underground and carried money and documents hidden in a basket.

Germany surrendered to the Allies in May 1945. World War II ended in August 1945. It was the largest and most destructive conflict in history.

After the war ended, the scattered remnants of the Jews of Poland and the rest of Europe attempted to pick up the pieces of their lives and continue on. Rachel Auerbach was among them. When it was all over, there were three survivors out of the 60 members who worked in some way with the Oyneg Shabes Archive: Rachel Auerbach, Hersh Wasser, and his wife, Bluma Wasser.

When the war ended, Rachel stayed in Warsaw and began working for the Jewish Historical Institute where she interviewed Holocaust survivors and preserved their stories in writing. In April 1946, Rachel spoke at a ceremony to remember the third anniversary of the Warsaw Ghetto Uprising. She was the only woman speaker. When she came to the podium, these were her words:

Remember, there is a national treasure under the ruins. The Ringelblum Archive is there. We cannot rest until we dig up the archive...

Even if there are five stories of ruins, we have to find the archive. I'm not making this up. I know what I'm talking about! This isn't just talk! This is coming from my heart. I will not rest, and I will not let you rest. We must rescue the Ringelblum Archive!

In spite of Rachel's message and challenge, there was not much of a response. After a world war, there were so many other problems. But Rachel stubbornly persisted.

Finally, in September 1946, the search for the Oyneg Shabes Archive began.

TWENTY-SEVEN

September 18, 1946
Warsaw, Poland

For weeks, workers had been searching. What had once been the Warsaw Ghetto was now nothing but blocks and blocks of debris and gutted buildings. There were no street signs or landmarks. Just finding where a certain street, building, or house had once been was hard enough; finding a cellar seemed impossible. The workers moved slowly and carefully, digging tunnels and pushing long metal stakes through the rubble. Rachel and Hersh knew the archive was there, but would it ever be found?

Day after day, the workers dug and excavated. And day after day, nothing was found. There just seemed to be too much space and too much destruction. But one day, a metal stake struck something underground. It didn't seem to be dirt or rocks, but something firmly in place. Digging with shovels, workers found a tin box tied with string. They kept digging and found nine more.

Rachel was already on her way to the Jewish Historical Institute. When she arrived, she was greeted with great

Rachel Auerbach and Hirsch Wasser unearthing part of the Ringelblum Archives, September 1946. Yad Vashem Photo Archives.

excitement! They had found the archive! In a room at the institute, Rachel and Hersh examined the ten boxes. As they lifted each mold-covered box, they could hear water inside. Would the documents and papers be ruined?

Carefully, they opened the first box. Rachel and Hersh stopped and looked at each other in amazement. There were the notebooks they had all been given for their essays and reports. Another box contained the last wills and testaments of those who had buried the archive: Israel, David, and Nahum. Another box contained underground newspapers, concert invitations, candy wrappers, poems, and drawings. All ten boxes had been found. Rachel and Hersh were overcome with emotion when they realized that Emanuel Ringelblum's mission had been successful and the world would know the truth.

But what about the buried milk cans? Polish construction workers found them four years later in December, 1950. The milk cans contained deportation notices, essays about the Great Deportation, and reports on the beginnings of resistance in the ghetto.

A third part of the archive, buried one week before the ghetto uprising, has never been found.

One of the three milk cans used by Warsaw ghetto historian Emanuel Ringelblum to store and preserve the secret "Oneg Shabbat" ghetto archives.

This milk can, identified as no. 2, was unearthed at 58 Nowolipki Street in Warsaw on December 1, 1950.

The milk can and casting of the Warsaw ghetto wall are displayed on the third floor of the permanent exhibition at the U.S. Holocaust Memorial Museum.

EPILOGUE

Present-Day
United States Holocaust
Memorial Museum, Washington, DC

A group of students stands before a glass-enclosed case at the United States Holocaust Memorial Museum in Washington, DC. The background is a brick wall, which was once part of the wall surrounding the Warsaw Ghetto. There are handwritten postcards and deportation notices. There is a painting.

Their eyes are drawn by a brighter light to a large metal milk can. It is covered in rust and dried dirt. The description that accompanies it mentions the Oyneg Shabes Archive, Emanuel Ringelblum, documents, artwork, and a building on 68 Nowolipki.

A quote beside the milk can reads::

I would love to live to see the moment in which the great treasure will be dug up and shriek to the world proclaiming the truth. So the world may know all...May the treasure fall into good hands, may it last into better times, may it alarm and alert the world to what happened and was played out in the twentieth century...We may now die in peace. We fulfilled our mission.

May history attest for us.
David Graber, 19 years old

In August 1942, during the Great Deportation in the Warsaw Ghetto, David Graber, Israel Lichtenstein, and Nahum Grzywacz worked until the last possible moments to bury the first part of the Oyneg Shabes Archive.

Thousands of Jews were being deported every day. They could hear gunfire and chaos in the street above them. They hurriedly wrote out what they knew could possibly be their last wills and testaments and put them in a tin box.

No one really knows exactly what happened to David, Nahum, Israel, and so many others imprisoned in the Warsaw Ghetto. But, in spite of his death, David's last wishes came true.

There was no way David could know, in August 1942, that decades later, his words and the words of many other courageous Jews in the Warsaw Ghetto would live on to tell this tragic, heroic story of Jewish cultural, spiritual, and personal resistance.

One of the metal milk cans is displayed in the permanent exhibition at the United States Holocaust Memorial Museum in Washington, DC.

The other milk can is part of the permanent exhibition at the Emanuel Ringelblum Jewish Historical Institute in Warsaw, Poland.

The original documents of the Oyneg Shabes Archive, over 6,000 of them, are housed in the Emanuel Ringelblum Jewish Historical Institute in Warsaw Poland.

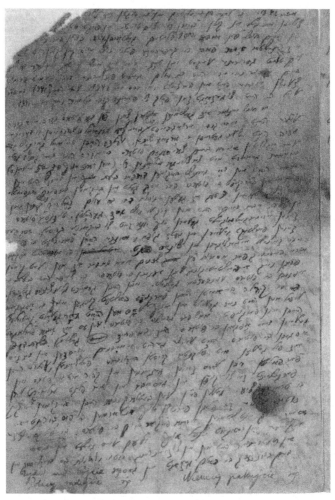

Page from Dr. Emanuel Ringelblum's writings. Found in Ringelblum Archive.
Courtesty of the Jewish Historical Institute in Warsaw, Poland.

INDEX

Fate of the Members of the Oyneg Shabes:

Emanuel Ringelblum: murdered by the Nazis on March 10, 1944, along with his wife, Judyta, and son Uri.

Israel Lichtenstein: last seen by Emanuel Ringelblum on April 19, 1943, on the first day of the Warsaw Ghetto Uprising; was probably killed by the Nazis while trying to make it back to his family's hideout on 68 Nowlipki Street or possibly deported to Treblinka.

David Graber: last seen on August 3, 1942; was probably killed by the Nazis in the Warsaw Ghetto during the Great Deportation or deported to Treblinka.

Nahum Grzywacz: last seen on August 3, 1942; was probably killed by the Nazis in the Warsaw Ghetto during the Great Deportation or deported to Treblinka.

Hersh Wasser: one of only three survivors of the Oyneg Shabes Archive.

Rachel Auerbach: one of only three survivors of the Oyneg Shabes Archive.

Also Mentioned In This Story:

Basia Berman: librarian in the Warsaw Ghetto. Escaped the Warsaw Ghetto in September 1942 and worked with the underground resistance on the Aryan side.

Halina Geldman: one of the top workers in Rachel Auerbach's soup kitchen in the Warsaw Ghetto. Deported and murdered in the gas chambers of Treblinka in August 1942.

Janusz Korczak: director of Jewish orphanage in the Warsaw Ghetto. On August 5 or 6, 1942, German authorities ordered Korczak, his staff, and around 200 children from the orphanage to board cattle cars to Treblinka. They were all murdered in the gas chambers upon arrival. He had repeatedly been offered shelter on the Aryan side, but said he could not abandon his children. Much is known and documented about his life, career and experiences in the Warsaw Ghetto.

Bluma Wasser: wife of Hersh Wasser. One of only three survivors of the Oyneg Shabes Archive.

Stefania Wilczynska: assistant to Janusz Korczak in the Jewish orphanage in the Warsaw Ghetto. On August 5 or 6, 1942, Wilczynska boarded the cattle cars with Korczak and around 200 children to Treblinka. They were all murdered in the gas chambers upon arrival. She was given the opportunity to evade the children's deportation, but chose to stay with the children.

Mieczyslaw Wolski: built the Krysia bunker at 81 Grojecka Street in Warsaw, Poland. Hid and gave shelter to over 30 Jews, including Emanuel Ringelblum and his family. When the hideout was discovered on March 4, 1944, Wolski and his nephew, Janusz Wysocki, were shot by the Germans.

On June 4, 1989, Wolski, his mother Malgorzata Wolska, his sisters, Halina Michalecka-Wolska and Wanda Szandurska-Wolska, and his nephew, Janusz Wysocki were recognized by Yad Vashem as Righteous Among the Nations.

WORKS CITED

Auerbach, Rachel. *Varshever Tsavoes (Warsaw Testaments)*. National Yiddish Book Center, 2002.

Jagur, Orna. *The Hiding Place*. Oficyna Bibliofilow, 2000.

Kassow, Samuel David. *Who Will Write Our History?: Rediscovering a Hidden Archive from the Warsaw Ghetto*. Vintage Books, 2009.

Kermish, Joseph. *To Live With Honor and Die With Honor! Selected Documents from the Warsaw Ghetto Underground Archives "O.S." ["Oneg Shabbath"]*. Yad Vashem, 1986.

Opochinsky, Peretz, et al. *In Those Nightmarish Days: the Ghetto Reportage of Peretz Opoczynski and Josef Zelkowicz*. Yale University Press, 2016.

Ringelblum, Emanuel, and Jacob Sloan. *Notes From the Warsaw Ghetto: The Journal of Emanuel Ringelblum*. Schocken Books, 1958.

Printed in Great Britain
by Amazon

23697307R00073